Sand cat

Cheetah

Wild cats come in many sizes.
A lion may be nine feet long
from its nose to the tip of its tail.
That is more than three times
longer than a house cat.
Here you can see what a house cat
looks like next to a lion, a lynx,
a sand cat, and a cheetah.

Wild Cats

by Peggy D. Winston

☐ BOOKS FOR YOUNG EXPLORERS
NATIONAL GEOGRAPHIC SOCIETY

COPYRIGHT © 1981 NATIONAL GEOGRAPHIC SOCIETY
LIBRARY OF CONGRESS CIP DATA: P. 32

A jaguar watches from a branch.

A tiger moves quietly through the forest.

Stripes cover its body from head to toe.

The big tiger and the little house cat

both belong to the family of cats.

Only the house cat is cuddly and tame.

The tiger and other cats are wild.

They run and climb, creep and pounce.

They growl and purr, nap and play.

All cats are much alike, as you will see.

Yet each kind is different, too.

Mountain lions

All cats have sharp claws.
A puma, or mountain lion,
scratches its claws on a log.
This helps keep them sharp.
Another mountain lion
runs along on strong legs.
When most cats walk or run,
their claws are pulled
inside their padded paws.

Lynx

A tiger shows long teeth
that grab and bite.
Its back teeth can tear meat.
Its pink tongue is rough,
like sandpaper.
The tiger uses its tongue
to lick its fur clean.
The lynx has thick fur
that keeps it warm
in the ice and snow.

Tiger

Lynx

A tiger shows long teeth
that grab and bite.
Its back teeth can tear meat.
Its pink tongue is rough,
like sandpaper.
The tiger uses its tongue
to lick its fur clean.
The lynx has thick fur
that keeps it warm
in the ice and snow.

Tiger

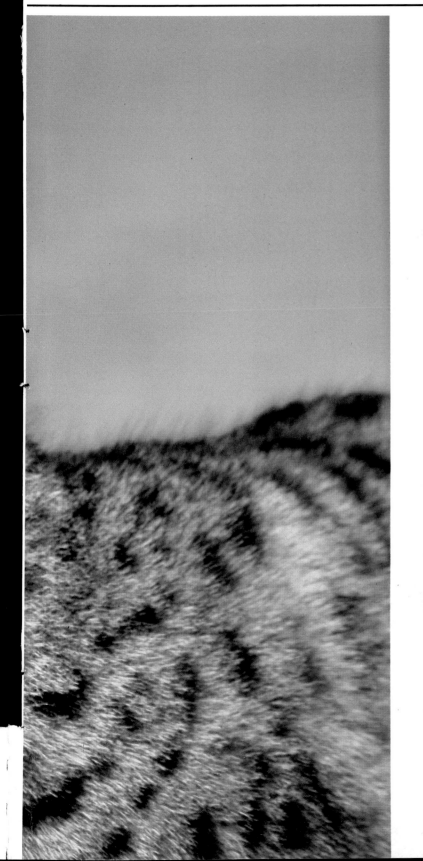

A furry bobcat watches and listens.
Its ears will catch the smallest sound.
The wide eyes of another wild cat
shine green in the night.
All cats see well in the dark.
Whiskers help them feel their way.
Sharp eyes and ears help wild cats hunt.
Wild cats eat meat. They must catch
and kill other animals for food.

Jaguarundi

A bobcat listens, looks, and digs.

What's moving under the snow?

Out pops a mouse. The chase begins!

With paws tucked under, a bobcat leaps

across the snow after a speedy hare.

Will the bobcat catch the hare?

Wild cats live in many places—
grassland, forest, mountain, and desert.
They often hide from animals they hunt.
They try to creep close without being seen.
Do you see the tiger standing here?
Its fur blends with the tall, dry grass.
The little wildcat in the forest
is also hard to see.
Its markings blend with the leaves.

European wildcat

Creep close, stop, and look.

Then attack with claws and teeth.

That is how most cats hunt.

A spotted serval stalks and stops.

Now the cat leaps to catch a hare.

A serval kitten begins to eat

while its mother cleans her paw.

A hungry bobcat goes fishing
in a rocky stream.
It puts out its paw
and slaps at a fish in the water.
Dripping wet, the bobcat comes ashore
with a meal in its jaws.

Cheetah chasing wildebeests

Getting food is hard work.
A cheetah can run very fast, but
the animals it hunts often get away.
A small cat, called a margay, and
a shy anteater meet on a branch.
Both animals look for food in trees.
Standing in a tree, a mountain lion
reaches up a prickly cactus plant.
A squirrel is hiding inside.

Anteater and margay

In the warm morning sun,
a young mountain lion looks out
from its resting place in the rock.
Its mother lies in the shade.

Clouded leopard

Caracals

Sand cat

Wild cats come in different sizes.

When tigers stand on their hind legs,

they are taller than most grown-ups.

The sand cat is as small as a house cat.

Wild cats look different from each other.

Some have spots or stripes or both.

And some have plain coats of fur.

The furry lynx, like most wild cats,

lives and hunts alone.

Lions are the only cats

that live and hunt in groups.

A group of lions is called a pride.

These female lions, or lionesses,

and their cubs have slept most of the day.

Now it is dusk. The lionesses will go out

on the flat, grassy plain to find food.

A lioness crouches low and drinks,
lapping with her tongue.
She has just finished a big meal.
Lions usually drink after eating.

Most tigers live in hot places.
They go swimming in rivers
and streams to cool off.
Splash! Two tigers play in the water.

Two cheetah cubs wrestle with each other.

Young wild cats spend a lot of time playing.

They chase and jump, slap and bite.

Playing like this helps them become hunters.

A mother cheetah stretches over her cubs.

When they are very young,

she cleans, feeds, and protects them.

Later, they learn to hunt on their own.

The male lion, with his fluffy mane,
does not usually go hunting.
Lionesses, like these with their cubs,
do most of the hunting for the pride.
They also take care of the cubs.
This lioness is moving her young cub
to a safe hiding place. She carries
the cub gently by the neck.

Some wild cats sleep in trees,
and some sleep on the ground.
House cats nap on rugs and chairs.
All cats spend much of the day
sleeping or resting.
A dozing lioness and her cub
lie among the top branches of a tree.
The big-eared cub is safe and snug
as it rests beside its mother.

Wild Cats
of the World

There are more than 30 kinds of wild cats.

One way of grouping them is by size.

As you can see, there are many more
small kinds than medium-size or large ones.

Small

1 Pampas cat
(say *PAM-puz*)

2 Black-footed cat

3 Chinese desert cat

4 European wildcat

5 Flat-headed cat

6 Geoffroy's cat
(*JEFF-reez*)

7 Iriomote cat
(*ear-ee-uh-MO-tay*)

8 Jaguarundi
(*JAG-wuh-RUN-dee*)

9 Jungle cat

10 Kodkod
(*CODE-code*)

11 Leopard cat
(*LEP-erd*)

12 Little-spotted cats

13 Marbled cats

14 Margay

15 Pallas's cat
(*PAL-us-ez*)

16 Rusty-spotted cat

17 Sand cat

Medium

18 Bobcat

19 Caracal
(CAR-uh-kal)

20 Fishing cat

21 Golden cat

22 Clouded leopard

23 Lynx
(LINKS)

24 Ocelot
(AH-suh-lot)

25 Serval
(SIR-vul)

26 Temminck's cat
(TEM-inks)

Large

27 Cheetah
(CHEE-tuh)

28 Jaguar
(JAG-wahr)

29 Leopard

30 Lions

31 Mountain lion

32 Snow leopard

33 Tiger

Staff and Illustrations Credits

Published by
The National Geographic Society
Gilbert M. Grosvenor, *President*
Melvin M. Payne, *Chairman of the Board*
Owen R. Anderson, *Executive Vice President*
Robert L. Breeden, *Vice President,*
 Publications and Educational Media

Prepared by
The Special Publications Division
Donald J. Crump, *Director*
Philip B. Silcott, *Associate Director*
William L. Allen, William R. Gray,
 Assistant Directors
Margery G. Dunn, *Managing Editor*
Gail N. Hawkins, *Researcher*

Illustrations and Design
Jim Abercrombie, *Picture Editor*
Constance B. Boltz, *Art Director*
Suez B. Kehl, *Associate Art Director*
Barbara Gibson, *Artist*
Katheryn M. Slocum, *Illustrations Assistant*

Engraving, Printing, and Product Manufacture
Robert W. Messer, *Manager*
George V. White, *Production Manager*
David V. Showers, *Production Project Manager*
Mark R. Dunlevy, Richard A. McClure, Raja D. Murshed,
 Christine A. Roberts, Gregory Storer,
 Assistant Production Managers
Mary A. Bennett, *Production Staff Assistant*

Debra A. Antonini, Nancy F. Berry, Pamela A. Black,
 Nettie Burke, Jane H. Buxton, Claire M. Doig,
 Rosamund Garner, Victoria D. Garrett, Virginia A. McCoy,
 Cleo Petroff, Victoria I. Piscopo, Tammy Presley,
 Carol A. Rocheleau, Jenny Takacs, *Staff Assistants*

Consultants
Dr. Glenn O. Blough, Peter L. Munroe, Adele S. Rammelmeyer,
 Karen O. Strimple, *Educational Consultants*
Lynda Ehrlich, *Reading Consultant*
Miles Roberts, Curator of Mammals, National Zoological Park;
 Dr. Ralph M. Wetzel, Professor of Biology, University of Connecticut,
 Scientific Consultants

Illustrations Credits
Tom McHugh, National Audubon Society Collection, Photo Researchers, cover, 4 lower, 23, 30 (6, 9, 13, 14), 31 (22, 29, 32); Francisco Erize, BRUCE COLEMAN INC., 1; George Holton, NASC/PR, 2–3; E. R. Degginger, BRUCE COLEMAN INC., 4 upper; Lee Foster, BRUCE COLEMAN INC., 5 left; John R. Lewis, TOM STACK & ASSOCIATES, 5 right; Tom McHugh, Wildlife Unlimited, NASC/PR, 6–7; Gary Milburn, TOM STACK & ASSOCIATES, 7; Stouffer Productions, ANIMALS ANIMALS, 8 upper, 8 lower, 12–13, 13 lower; Marty Stouffer, 8–9; George B. Schaller, BRUCE COLEMAN INC., 10–11; Russ Kinne, NASC/PR, 11, 12, 13 upper right; A. A. Geertsema, 13 upper; Thomas Nebbia, DPI, Inc., 14 upper; Warren Garst, TOM STACK & ASSOCIATES, 14 lower, 26 lower; E. R. Degginger, 15, 21, 31 (23, 24, 27); Wolfgang Bayer, 16–17; D. & R. Sullivan, BRUCE COLEMAN INC., 18; Jeanne White, NASC/PR, 19 center, 31 (19); Stouffer Enterprises, ANIMALS ANIMALS, 19 lower; Tom McHugh, Chicago Zoological Park, NASC/PR, 19 upper, 31 (22); Jon A. Hull, BRUCE COLEMAN INC., 20–21; George B. Schaller, New York Zoological Society, 22 upper; E. Hanumantha Rao, NASC/PR, 22 lower; George W. Frame, 24; Sven-Olof Lindblad, NASC/PR, 25; M. Philip Kahl, NASC/PR, 26 upper, 31 (28, 31); Jen and Des Bartlett, 26–27; Susan McCartney, NASC/PR, 28–29; Tom McHugh, Cincinnati Zoo, NASC/PR, 30 (1, 5, 12); Anthony Bannister, NHPA, 30 (2); Peking Zoological Gardens (Peking Zoo), 30 (3); Hans Reinhard, BRUCE COLEMAN INC., 30 (4); Tadaaki Imaizumi, Orion Press, 30 (7); C. Allan Morgan, 30 (8); Louie Psihoyos, 30 (10); M.P.L. Fogden, BRUCE COLEMAN INC., 30 (11); Anthony Blueman, Root Resources, 30 (15, 17); Janet Ross, Cincinnati Zoo, 30 (16); Leonard Lee Rue III, 31 (18); Stanley Breeden, 31 (20); G. D. Plage, BRUCE COLEMAN INC., 31 (21); Christina Loke, NASC/PR, 31 (25); G. D. Dodge & D. R. Thompson, BRUCE COLEMAN INC., 31 (26); Mohamed Ismail, NASC/PR, 31 (30); Zig Leszczynski, ANIMALS ANIMALS, 31 (33); Loren McIntyre, 32.

Library of Congress CIP Data
Winston, Peggy D.
 Wild cats.

 (Books for young explorers)
 Summary: Brief text and photographs present the physical characteristics and behavior of various kinds of wild cats.
 1. Felidae—Juvenile literature. [1. Felidae. 2. Cats] I. National Geographic Society (U. S.) II. Title. III. Series.
QL737.C23W56   599.74′428   81-44742
ISBN 0-87044-401-8 (regular binding)   AACR2
ISBN 0-87044-406-9 (library binding)

A panting jaguar rests in a tree.
Cover: *A caracal mother guards her young.*

Lion

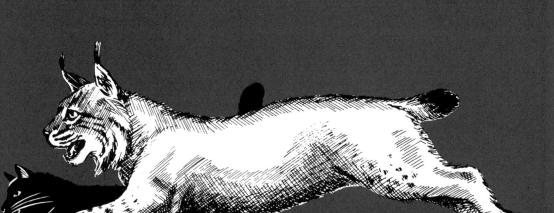

Lynx